Who Are You?

Melanie Daynes

Presentation by *BookLeaf Publishing*

Web: www.bookleafpub.com

E-mail: info@bookleafpub.com

ISBN: 9789357441087

First edition 2023

DEDICATION

For Joshua.

For being the best inspiration of all.

Who Are You?

When someone asks, 'Who are you?'
What do you do?
Do you think of your height, your hair, your
health?
Your job, your kids, your wealth?
Your weight, your hobby, your day?
What do you say?

'Who am I?' you ask
Answering that is not an easy task
I am a daughter, a mother
A wife like no other
A sister, a friend
I seem to have no end

I am the colleague you like
Who works through the night
The colleague you don't
And most probably won't
The worker who stays
Till the end of the day

I am ordering a coffee
Or maybe a latte
And a cake, too

How about you?
Then I'll sit at a table
Because I am able

I am tall
If you are small
I am small
If you are tall
But if I recall
I am my own height after all

I am the mother at the school gate
Wondering what her child has ate
The one chatting with others
Talking with another mother
About our childrens' likes
While waiting for our little tikes

I have a father and a mother
Two sisters and a brother
A big family with laughter
And sore ribs after
One niece and many nephews
Their cuteness, I can't refuse

I am rich
Being alive is rich
I am healthy
I am lucky to be healthy

I am poor
But I'm sure I am more

I am all
And none of them are small
Because I am me
And I am free
To be myself
And no one else

So when someone with a view
Asks 'Who are you?'
Say, 'I thought you knew
Of me there are few
Can't you see?
I am me'

Today

Today has been a good day
Filled with laughter and love
My son was running around
Being a kid is just enough
My brother was sharing stories
Of his work and his friends
One of my sisters was chatting
About days that never seem to end
My father was thinking
Of working in his shed
My mother was fussing and cooking
Making sure we are all well fed
My other sister was running around
After her youngest child
While my niece was giggling shouting
Making us all think she was wild
Two nephews were discussing game plays
On computer consoles
While the other nephew tried hard
To not make his eyes roll
The dog has been chasing her tail
As well as barking
The budgie has been chirping loudly
It sounded more like harking
The noise filled the air of the house

To an almost deafening level
For anyone outside
It all must sound like the devil
Yes, today has been a good day
Filled with all my family
Although they are not mine through choice
I would still choose them quite happily
For they have made me who I am
They have helped me to grow
They are all the best family
A fact I would like them to know

Your Name

Your name is such a funny thing
It often pops into your head
When asked the simple question
Who are you?

Your name belongs you
Yet is used by everyone else
It always feels very personal
When someone says your name

Your name has a meaning
That could be used to describe
You and all that you are
If it is true to you

Your name can be changed
Made longer or shorter
Depending on the person speaking it
And where you are

Your name was discussed
Before you were born
By your parents as they uncovered
The best name for you

Your name is called
Throughout your life
You learn to respond to it
With a smile or a nod

Your name could be native
Or it could be foreign
But whichever it is
It is perfect for you

Your name is unique to you
No one else owns it
It is a part of you
And who you are

To My Son

To my son
Who made me a parent
Who came as a surprise
That was quite apparent

A surprise you were
But you were never unwanted
An amazing gift
And I was simply daunted

You came very quickly
With no instructions
And whose tiny little bed
Took lots of construction

You would wake in the night
Wanting feeding and cuddles
And I tiredly obliged
Even though my brain was a muddle

Everyone would tell me
How beautiful you are
And I would agree
As you are my star

Learning to walk
And stumble along
As your tired little legs
Were not that strong

Talking, chatting, giggling
You soon learned them all
While I started to notice
That you were getting tall

Starting school was quite a big thing
You walked happily into a crowd
And starting chatting with glee
And attracted more children from all around

Making friends and getting along
You are very good at those
At school you are popular
And it really shows

Reading books at bedtime
Watching you open presents
All of these little things
For which I'm glad I'm present

I wouldn't change a single day
That you made me a mother
I know I am blessed
And wouldn't choose another

You helped to shape me
Into who I am today
And I am one of the lucky ones
Who had a child to stay

I want to thank you, my son
For being my shining star
I am tall and strong
Because of who you are

You are beautiful and kind
And I just wanted to say
You are part of me forever
And not just for today

I look forward to meet
The person you grow to be
As I'm sure you will be
An adult amazingly

One Word

One word may be all it takes
To make your day
Or turn it around

One word may help you grow
To give you courage
So you conquer it all

One word can be like love
That fills you with warmth

One word can be like sadness
That consumes you completely

One word may open doors
And gives you wings
And strength to stand tall

One word does not say a lot
About you
Or who you are

One word can be one part of you
Inside or outside

Yet not wholly you

One word is just that
A simple word and not fact

One word can help to explain
Your day, your week, your year
But not completely who you are

One word is not you
You are more than just words
You are you

Empty Hours

What do you like to do
In your spare time?

Do you like to draw?
Or maybe you like to write

What are your thoughts on stamps?
And making lots of cards

Is there a favourite television show?
Filled with your favourite stars?

Do you trawl through stalls on a Sunday?
And find forgotten treasures.

Maybe knitting is your thing
Along with sewing for pleasure.

I like to read a good book
And find writing a joy

Do you enjoy swimming, like me
I like to keep fit with my boy

Are you good at crosswords?

They can be a challenge

And those who like dancing
Have some very good talent

Weight lifting is good for some
Others like to run

I hear of all kinds of hobbies
And they all sound like fun

There are many exciting pastimes
And whatever you like to do

To help you relax and unwind
Is just the hobby for you

To Other People

To every stranger I pass
I try to be kind
By offering a smile
As well as a greeting

To my friends
I try to chat a little
About how life is today
And when we can next meet

To my son
I try lead by example
Teach him right from wrong
And support his choices

To my husband
I try to keep smiling
To look forward to the future
And growing old together

To my parents
I try to make them proud
And check on them each week
To see if they are well

To my siblings
I try to keep in touch
Visit their homes
Ask about their families

To my colleagues
I try to be helpful
And catch up on the chatter
From their weekends' ventures

To my life
I try to live it my way
As much as I can
With happiness everywhere

I Believe

For all the people in the world
We don't all agree
On the same God or Gods
Or other deity

For some it is one God
For others, it is several
A God or Goddess
Or even a devil

Some believe in guardian angels
While others believe that
The universe will look after them
And will have their backs

Your beliefs are your own
They are personal everyone
Some people take them seriously
While others just have fun

It is okay to have your own belief
And to live in peace
As beliefs can help your worries
And your concerns to cease

The Mirror

If I looked into a mirror
What do I see?
I may say I was tall

Brown eyes that smile
And hair that changes
Depending on my mood

My weight, I have have no idea
It changes over the year
Especially over Christmas

I sometimes wear glasses
I sometimes look smart
I sometimes wear old clothes

This is just what I believe
I look like outside

If you looked into the mirror
What would you see?

Because it doesn't really matter
What clothes you wear

Or the colour of your hair

These words do not describe you
As they do not define
Who you are completely

Writing Every Day

Today I didn't feel like writing
I just wanted to stay in bed
And try not let my thoughts
Fill me with complete dread

Today I didn't feel like writing
I just wanted to sit and read
What others had written before me
And how they had managed to succeed

Today I didn't feel like writing
I just found it quite hard
To write what I was feeling
Straight from the heart

Today I didn't feel like writing
I just felt too worried
About what others would think of my words
And if they were too hurried

Today I didn't feel like writing
I just picked up my pen
And started doodling on paper
While counting up to ten

Today I didn't feel like writing
I just found I was forming words
On the paper in front of me
Creating chapters and verse

Today I didn't feel like writing
I just realised after a time
A page of a story had appeared
And that story was mine

Today I didn't feel like writing
But I still wrote all the same
And before I knew what had happened
The words appeared from flames

Seasons

My mood is like the seasons
That changes all the time
One minute it can be rainy
And followed by sunshine

I want to be alone
And filled with all my thoughts
Then I want to be with people
In whose gossip I am caught

I feel sad for no reason
Want to cry with real tears
But then I will feel happy
And believe I could be for years

I need to exercise and run
Be strong and lift weights
The next day however
A pizza will fill my plate

One day, I'd like to run through fields
In the sunshine, feeling free
The next day, I'm at home
With biscuits and a cup of tea

I am different from one day to the next
I wear a smile, and then a frown
It is who I am
And it doesn't get me down

Fresh Air

A walk in the park
May just be what you need
To pick up your mood
And make you smile with ease

Grinning at strangers
As you walk on by
With a nod of your head
And a glance with your eye

Hearing the birds singing
As they're perched on branches
The rustling of leaves
As the wind dances

The scurry of a squirrel
The hop of a rabbit
Watching the wildlife
Go about their daily habits

Yes, a walk in the park
Is exactly what I require
And after the wander
To my home I retire

Working Day

Dropping off my son
At the school gates
So he can
Learn with his friends

Arriving at the office
I pull up a chair
Turn on the computer
And plan my day

Will it be busy?
Will it be quiet?
Are there many emails?
What about the phone?

Say hello to my colleagues
Ask about their weekend
Check if they need a drink
Or a bite to eat

Typing, printing, writing
Writing, chatting, walking
The working day
Is underway

Quick drink, quick lunch
Quick walk in the fresh air
Then back to the office
To finish up the day

Walking to the car
Working day done
Thinking about dinner time
And what we have to cook

Driving through traffic
Lights, stop, start
Turn left, turn right
Waiting for cars to pass

Pulling up at the school
To collect my son from class
He tells me stories of his day
And the friends he saw

Opening the front door
Breathing a sigh of relief
It's good to be home
The end of the working day

Being Anxious

We are all told
That worrying does nothing
But steal your happiness
And waste your time

It causes tears and sadness
And costs your friendships
It does nothing to help you
Does not make you happy

But I can't help but worry
About my son and his life
About my life and my work
Is it good enough?

I have since found out
That lots of worrying
Is not good for you

Lots of worrying
Is worrying in itself

If you worry lots
Ask a friend
To help you unload

Separation

When two people meet
And get along well
It's almost as if
They are under a spell

They may plan their future
And where they want to live
How many children they'd like to have
And what will have to give

Gathering furniture and utensils
Both functional and for pleasure
The home they are making
Becomes theirs at their own leisure

Painting and building
Hammering and soothing
Their lives connected
And their relationship moving

One day the same people wake up
With no love in their heart
For the person they lie next to
They may want to be apart

Separating their lives that were once intertwined
Heads heavy with sadness
The future looks uncertain
As if filled with blackness

The blackness will stop
The skies will become blue
Once again their lives
With start anew

A life no longer together
Both living apart
But one thing is clear
Deep inside their hearts

They are happier away
One separate from the other
They will move on
A new life they will discover

Ourselves

f you could be an animal
What would you choose?

A dog, loyal as can be
A cat, independently climbing a tree
A rabbit, whose soft fur you can feel
A hamster, running fast on a wheel
A bird, happily singing a song
A squirrel, whose tail is fluffy and long
A snake, slithering on the grass
A cheetah, racing past fast
A lion, standing tall and proud
Or a human, getting lost in a crowd

It is funny how we use animals
To describe ourselves

As Strong as an ox
Or cunning like a fox

When we all have our own
Charisma and charm

Strangers

I wonder who that man is
Walking his dog along the road
On the way to the park

What is his name?
Where does he work?
Is that his dog?

I wonder who that woman is
Driving her nice car
Along the busy main street

Where is she going?
Where has she been?
Is she having a good day?

I wonder who those teens are
Standing in a crowd
In the middle of town

Do they all know each other?
Do they go to school together?
What are their thoughts for the future?

Strangers are all around us

We see them every day
But we don't always notice them
Even when they look our way

We are all living our lives
Together on this earth
So maybe we should be kind
For what it's worth

Kind to each other as all of us
Go about our daily lives
Maybe we should smile more
And give each other high fives

Puzzle Pieces

I am the puzzle
Of which all the pieces
When put together
Make all of me

My family, my son
My husband, my friends
My colleagues, my looks
My anxiety are all one blend

All of them are bits of wool
Sewn together with perfect stitches
To show the world who I am
And every one of my riches

My pieces are unique
They belong to me
Each one is not the same
As individual as can be

Everyone is their own jigsaw
Built piece by piece
Clicking perfectly into place
Without a crease
No one is the same

We are our own selves
Our uniqueness is what makes us
Each of us being ourself.